SÃO MIGUEL

AZORES

SÃO MIGUEL AZORES **(3rd EDITION)**

EDITOR
Ver Açor, Lda.

EDITORIAL COORDENATION
Ver Açor, Lda.

PHOTOGRAPHY
© Ver Açor, Lda.*
Nuno Sá
Fernando Resendes

TEXT BY
Daniel de Sá

TRANSLATION
Chrys Chrystello

GRAPHIC DESIGN
Ver Açor, Lda.
Helder Segadães

IMAGE TREATMENT
Ver Açor, Lda.
Paulo Cabral

FINAL ARTWORK
Ver Açor, Lda.

PRE-PRINT_PRINTING
Gráfica Maiadouro, S.A.

LEGAL DEPOSIT
Nº 354277/13

ISBN
978-989-8123-14-5

Ponta Delgada, february 2013

* Except
Eng. Francisco Botelho, Pag. 9 (Left)

Published by Ver Açor, Lda.
Rua da Boa Nova, 80
9500-296 Ponta Delgada - Açores
Tel./Fax 296 684 926 - Mobile Phone 913 461 799
veracor@veracor.pt
www.veracor.pt

açoresnatural
SÃO MIGUEL
AZORES
veraçor
editores

SÃO MIGUEL MAP

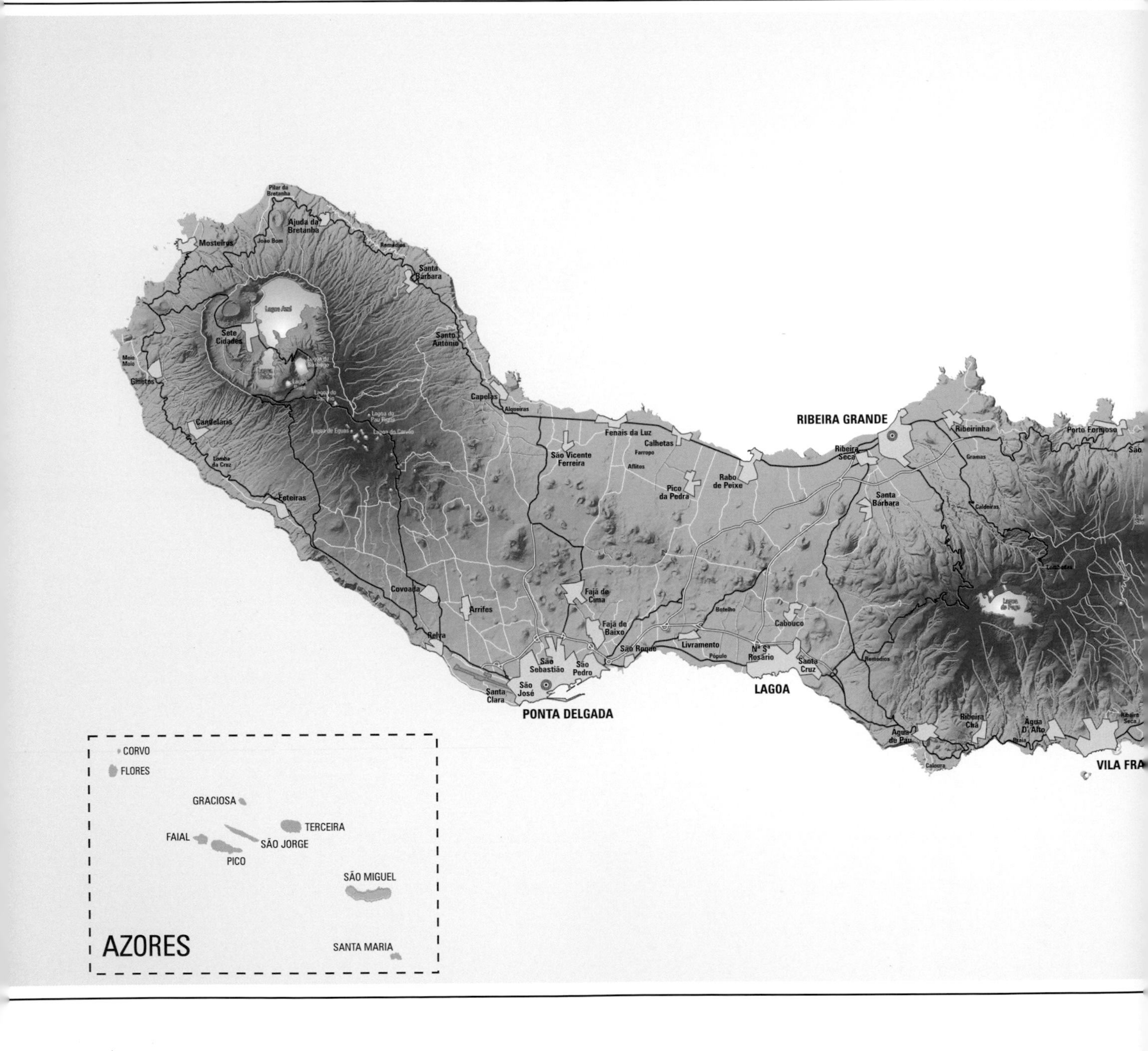

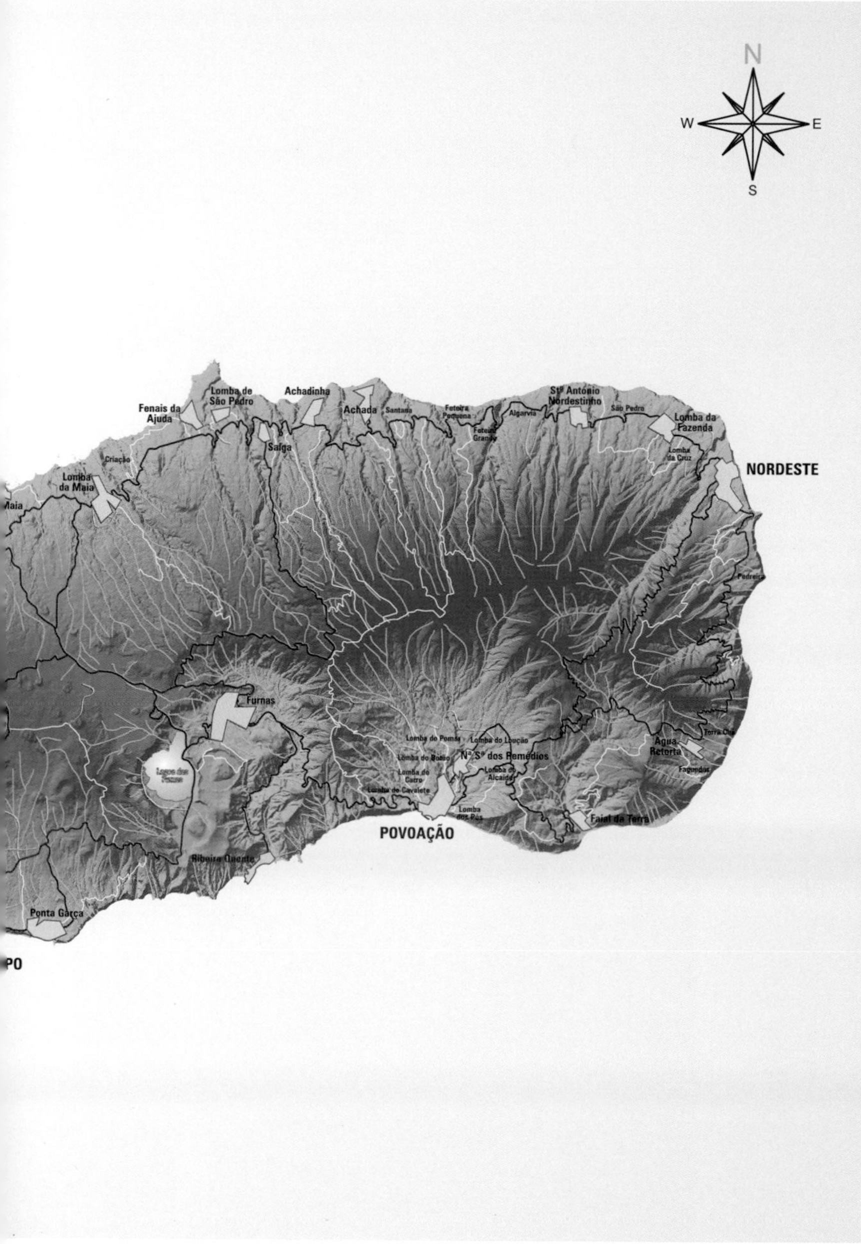

TABLE OF CONTENTS

NORDESTE

Those were the days when Nordeste was still afar. On dry weather, from the gravel road used to travel within the county, flew away a yellowish, constant and fine dust. Anything or anyone moving on it would mark its passage raising clouds of dust. Insidiously, they would persist if no breeze spread them on top of haystacks, against houses, valleys and hills.
The traveller went past the village for the first time, past Lomba da Pedreira, a yearlong crèche. Next day he would stroll through its streets as a Bethlehem shepherd. The most unexpected surprise of all surprises came a few kilometres away when the road became wider and in macadam. He had left behind the "barrocais", those valleys eroded by rain and by those mythical Nordeste creeks - Woman Creek, Undress When You Sweat Creek and William Creek -... The imposing cliffs of Achada, Feteiras and Algarvia were lost amidst the thousand bends of the road and the landscape... Around these parts, the island was cut by deep seas as in a picture frame. Seemed like an odd couple in bad terms, only touching at the edge of the cliffs per chance and with dislike, as if the island and the seas had nothing in common.
From the asphalted road, the traveller is unaware of the prodigious work of those who put it so far away, in the most improbable of all places. He will not be able to see any other living soul using the road or watching it. From the road, one can discover a stranger and more fascinating world just there, where the island started being formed four million years ago: everything happens as at the climax of a symphonic poem when the refrain echoes and thunders repeatedly throughout the entire orchestra. Each bend of the road, the traveller seeks the difference. It comes out suddenly in the awe of a creek coming down from where the Vara Peak reaches for the skies. There, where the priolo (Azores Bullfinch), one of the rarest birds on earth, hides in its camouflaged vest, mimicking the clouds and the shadows.
The traveller suddenly stops; someone from his group says, "Shush". There was no need; the only one who dared speak was the one begging for silence.
In awe, he mulls over, not knowing the name of that creek. It comes down from the mountain in a rush to break away from the heights of Tronqueira. Then, it slows down a bit and the geological fault where it drops to the sea widens and spares no space. All types of trees that dot the island embellish those banks down to the riverbed that no one can see. Thousands of birds chant as in a final bouquet. Not even one to be seen. One cannot distinguish their voices echoing from all places in unison...

Pedreira, the hill of the raising Sun.

Pico da Vara. From the top of this mountain, we stare at four million years.

Santana.
Feteira Pequena and Feteira Grande

Achada. This churchyard is one of the most beautiful belvederes in the island.

Later, he will learn its name, Caimbos Creek. Apparently, the first people to cross it in bygone days used some hooks to grab at the banks when escalating them. As for the road that first got him surprised, he was told it was the work of Park Rangers who have perhaps performed in Nordeste some of the most nature-loving acts of all these islands. (One day they will build a belvedere, worth a fairy tale, in the Bartholomew peak where the creek is born)

The traveller forgets the sad beauty of all small villages he went past. They all had the colour of the grey winter days. As if there was never sunshine or moonlight during those long nights. However, he loves them in their old modesty, delighted with the contrasts of their smallness when compared to the vastness of the landscape. He is sure everything will change although he could not foresee it would be as much and so fast. Those people hurt for being alive! Nevertheless, they all possess a natural finesse coupled with a solid upbringing as much bonded to their souls as the urze (Erica azorica) and the queirós (Calluna vulgaris) are attached to the steepest and inaccessible ravines. Many a year later, even graziers and their cattle shall walk past the asphalted roads. The sad and grey beauty will be replaced by a permanent colour festival. The traveller will never stop being amazed by the flowers bordering the tracks, houses and backyards or, even, covering the trunks of palm trees at the village of Fazenda, and from Salga, with its kaleidoscopic gardens up to the apotheosis of the town of Nordeste,. Doubts will arise when thinking how to go from Nordeste to Água Retorta. One can go from tip to tip – down from the oldest lighthouse in the Azores at Arnel guiding the sailors since 1876, to Marquesa, Sossego, Madrugada – or risking to almost touch the island's pinnacle at the belvedere or mirage of Tronqueira.

Santo António de Nordestinho.
These beautiful stones have been praying for us for over a century.

Climbing up **Pico da Vara**, the pinnacle of the island.

Priolo, a kind of bullfinch,
is a true *avis rara* that only lives in this small world.

Today's houses missing the past.

Arnel Lighthouse.
Beaming the sailors' life since 1876.

Here, we never loose the skyline neither the eyes.

Foz da Ribeira. Salt-water pool.

Ribeira dos Caldeirões. Natural park.

Ponta do Sossego. The sea stops and the island climbs.

POVOAÇÃO

On a long detour by the foothills of Lombo Gordo, and once past the Caimbos Creek, the traveller moves into another county, although the landscape dismisses such fact and remains the same. Mountains to the right and seas to the left. Ravines, cliffs and precipices. Always between the fright and the dream. Then, one arrives at Água Retorta, or goes through there to Água Retorta, to be welcomed by those who had left the county of Povoação, a league earlier. Were it a bird or the wind and the distance would be halved. The land is much crinkled and rough to walk on, but so soft for the eyes, before suddenly descending abruptly into the seas, where the revolute waters fall. They are from a creek whose name extended to the village. It looks like two places. In flat lowland areas, there is the nucleus of the village surrounding the church of Our Lady of Penha de França, and above it, another village developed conforming to the constraints of the terrain. The traveller does not feel tired. Each recess glimpsed acts as a prize for the length of the journey. Another league gone and one reaches the road going down to Faial da Terra. A trip with return, twisting back and forth to avoid being totally perpendicular. Suddenly, the land becomes flat, a small fajã[1] crossed by a creek dividing the village into two. Turning one's back to the sea brings daydreams of being in the Alps. The waves do not need to spatter very high to wet the land close

by. Were they more emboldened and surely they could kneel at the doorstep of the Nossa Senhora da Graça (Our Lady of Graces) Church.

A dozen houses are scattered through the hills, soon to be emptied by the passage of time and inclemency of weather. Its ravage will disembowel and blind the windows leaving the doors ajar. It is the village of Sanguinho. Later, all those houses will be recovered, rehabilitated, caulked, electrified and plumbed. Therefore, they can pretend being what they once were in order to well receive tourists. It does not

[1]flat lowland areas formed by lava flowing into the ocean and landslides and collapsing cliffs.

matter, since Mother Nature will remain the same, millenary. Only poets, hermits or paupers could have lived there.

The next descent will be well inside the collapsed caldera where Povoação lies. (Well, what is a collapsed caldera? That is what happens then the insides of a volcanic cone abruptly fell due to withdrawal of magmatic chambers). The traveller stops at Pico Longo to contemplate the scenery. Or, at what is left of such caldera that the seas have smashed on the south side. A spectacular grandeur, whose major scenario comes down in the shape of "lombas" (humps) from the Peak of Vara and the tablelands of Graminhais. The landscape goes as far away as the eyes can see, or until one gets lost in the scenery. Someone tries to tell the name of these and all the other "lombas" which surround it from east to west, each completed or crowned by a small village. He goes on finger counting them and misses one: Carro (Car). Repeats the counting and the mistake. This time, he forgot another one: Botão (Button). Then he goes on with the rigmarole, saying all seven of them without mistake either in number or in order: Pós (Powder), Alcaide (Mayor),

Cows are almost sovereign around the island

Pico Longo Belvedere - a world at your feet

Loução (Gracious), Pomar (Orchard), Botão (Button), Carro (Car), Cavaleiro (Knight).
The road coming down to the village crosses through Lomba do Alcaide. Down there, not far from the creek that has caused many a tragedy, the first colonisers set foot on this island, perhaps in front of where the old Mother Church still resists. The traveller glimpses at the waves as if staring at an historical monument. It was there that the first village took shape and the first human being was born. For a while, being the only one, the place did not need another name, which it has kept throughout the times: Povoação (literally meaning village). Sometimes it was known as Nova Povoação (New Village). When others were established, it became known as Povoação Velha (old village), but soon returned to its simpler, almost pagan, baptismal name.
Climbing up Lomba do Cavaleiro, the quiet sights of grandeur are reiterated. Up there, probably where the first chapel in the island was built, remains the Saint Barbara Little Chapel. Although this was the first settlement in the island of São Miguel, Povoação only

Faial da Terra - far away but absolutely worth it

Povoação - It is alleged that here the discoverers and the colonisers first disembarked

Lagoa das Furnas - Chromatic variations on a water theme

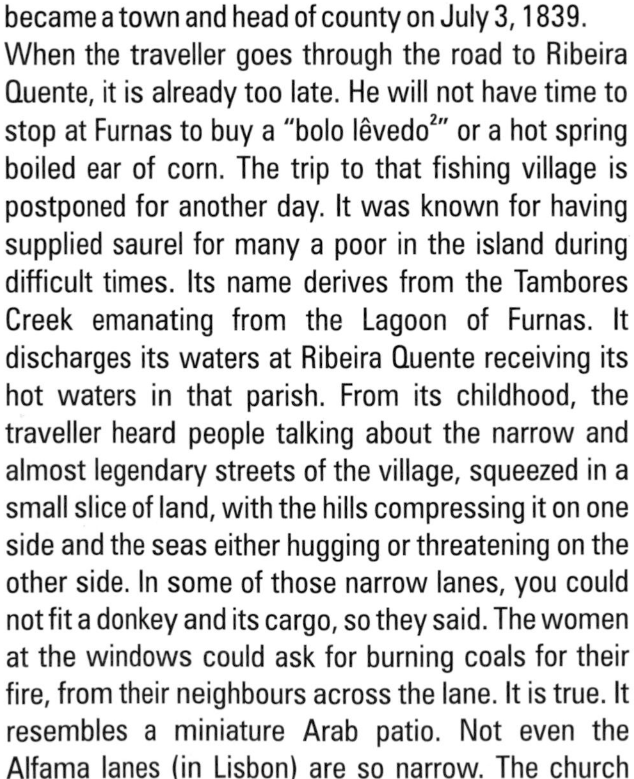

became a town and head of county on July 3, 1839. When the traveller goes through the road to Ribeira Quente, it is already too late. He will not have time to stop at Furnas to buy a "bolo lêvedo[2]" or a hot spring boiled ear of corn. The trip to that fishing village is postponed for another day. It was known for having supplied saurel for many a poor in the island during difficult times. Its name derives from the Tambores Creek emanating from the Lagoon of Furnas. It discharges its waters at Ribeira Quente receiving its hot waters in that parish. From its childhood, the traveller heard people talking about the narrow and almost legendary streets of the village, squeezed in a small slice of land, with the hills compressing it on one side and the seas either hugging or threatening on the other side. In some of those narrow lanes, you could not fit a donkey and its cargo, so they said. The women at the windows could ask for burning coals for their fire, from their neighbours across the lane. It is true. It resembles a miniature Arab patio. Not even the Alfama lanes (in Lisbon) are so narrow. The church

[2]muffin-like pancake.

Furnas - Lord walks over the colourful splendour of its Creation when visiting the sick and the infirm,*(Left)*

Furnas were initially inhabited by hermits *(Center, Top)*

Boiling water from the hot springs...
... and running down a creek where hot and cold waters mix *(Center, Bottom)*

Plane trees *(platanus hispanica)* were devastated during the orange exportation period *(Right, Bottom)*

consecrated to São Paulo (St Paul's) is now on a vantage point, well protected from stormy sea waves, which previously have destroyed the two preceding churches. Until the 20th century, to get to the village you had to go by sea. In 1936 and in 1940, the first and only two road tunnels in the island of S. Miguel were dug in. Years later, the traveller discovers a disturbing optical illusion. He may want to repeat such experience many times. After the second tunnel, and once past the bend, you get the absolute feeling that you are still descending half way through the straight-line road. However, were you to stop and get the clutch into neutral gear, the car would start going backwards at an impressive speed.

The village has a splendid and famous beach. It is surrounded by high cliffs and it is naturally warmed in some spots thanks to hydrothermal springs a few meters from the shoreline. Most of the land where the village lies comes from the 1588 landslide and the volcanic eruption of 1630. It is also one of the villages, which has lost more population in the past decades of the 20th century. In 1965, it had 2421 inhabitants and that number was down to 798 in the 2001 Census.

Slow-cooking a stew inside the volcano, also seasoned by a slight taste of sulphur

The beautiful ugliness of the volcanic hot springs

Ribeira Quente - "House, how many can live inside" and street, how many do you fit in?

A waterfall is the sign language of water

Natural Park **Terra Nostra**, the most exquisite in the archipelago was created by Thomas Hickling, the first USA Consul in the Azores

THE WATER CIRCUS THE THREE-LAGOON PILGRIM

This would surely be the best way to know the world, if only one could walk all over it. As it becomes easier to reach inaccessible villages, many times we tend to discard those who are closer by.

The traveller has already befriended the most famous lagoons through that old-fashioned manner of unhurriedly walking through the pathways of the island. It might be a protracted but not less fascinating journey. First, he went to Sete Cidades, starting at Feteiras do Sul with a couple of friends. Every little bit of the way up ought to be admired although no one is ever prepared for the revelation of such splendour. One might have seen a thousand pictures and

documentaries but none can imitate reality. The space is huge; the silence seems to muffle even the occasional noises, as the green from the hills. The pinnacles blend with the blue from the skies and the seas in the most abstruse and perfect harmony. The mysterious, mythical and legendary twin lagoons are down there, in the middle of that ancient crater which

became a caldera. One is green and reflects the colours from its bottom and the slopes; the other is blue and mirrors the sky. In those distant days, the colours were still clear-cut and not obfuscated by the change of bread making fields into wealthy milk farms.

The mountain range of Sete Cidades (Seven Cities) is not the only jewel in the crown of these lagoons. There are, at least, another dozen jewels in the mere space of a league further southwest, being the most notorious the Santiago Lagoon (St James) and the Canário Lagoon (Canary or Finch). The ancient chronicler Gaspar Frutuoso, wrote respectfully yet timorous about it, a century after the settlement. He adds a small detail in tones of mystery, as to its depth amongst thick brushes, stating that in its waters "it was found a certain type of fish, looking like a prawn but stuck to a wooden stick". The Canário Lagoon, surrounded by vegetation where moss and groves of trees abound, feeds Ponta Delgada with its water. Frutuoso calls it "Canários" (finches) Lagoon, explaining that its name does not derive from the canorous birds that only arrived later on. In those bygone days, on its environs, people from the Canary Islands used to take some sheep and goats to pasture. Once the archipelago given to Gullén de las Casas was baptised, at almost the same time as the discovery of this island, it gave name not only to those birds (and they came from there) but also to this lagoon.

Those were the days when the traveller's legs did ache less ascending than now descending. On the return, when reaching Vista do Rei, where HRH Dom Carlos stopped in July 1901 and thus gave name to the Royal Belvedere, the three travellers were indeed tired. As exhausted and thirsty as Roman Legionnaires who had run into vinegar instead of water in their flasks. It was, then, in that place where so many miracles occur that they witnessed yet another one. They saw, at large, a man drawing milk from the udder of a cow. God only knows how much they wanted to have a sip of milk. As if the man could have read their minds or wishes, the shepherd, farmer or angel, called out for them to come close by. He served them on top of the tin all the lukewarm milk they wanted! May St Nicholas have protected him for the rest of his natural life.

Sete Cidades - amidst such a scenery no one wonders why this is a place for legends

His second trip to one of the three most famous lagoons on S. Miguel was in a larger group, but they all lost their will and gave up even before departing.
To go to Furnas everybody is more than rewarded by any sacrifice needed to get there. It is one of the most renowned, studied and prestigious places in the world. You can hardly say anything new about such place, since it has already been said before. It is thus impossible to try to create a new language. The grandeur of the whole place is understood or ascertained when one looks for a high and distant vantage point surrounding it. The most widely visited is Pico do Ferro, on top of a ravine coming abruptly almost to the shore of the lagoon. The spectacular, phenomenon or phenomena, heightens its splendour when seen from Salto do Cavalo (Horse Jump) or from the heights of Castelo Branco (White Castle). Furnas is a place one cannot say or describe how it is, but has to go and see what is.

The beauty of **Furnas** and the peaceful walk of the pilgrims on their way to the small chapel of Nossa Senhora das Vitórias (Our Lady of Victories), on the western bank of the lake.

For the third of these pilgrimages, the traveller left Chã do Rego de Água, between Lagoa and Ribeira Grande. He was on a military camping expedition with a friend from Pico Island. The more they climbed the more the island seemed to grow. It looked like it was lying down to the North and spreading elongated to the South. The walk was long but each step made it worthy, as if there was no need to go any further to fulfil the senses. Each time, it became more primitive, more savage and more pure. Suddenly, it became no more than moss and queirós (Calluna vulgaris). A last breadth and the road revealed the Barrosa Peak. The lagoon was close by. It is called the Fire Lagoon; since it was there, that, the sleepy volcano woke up in 1563. In those days, the feared and fascinating vital manifestations from the Earth were called fire, as in bushfire.
A few more steps. There it was. The dream. The enchantment. The doubt between real and imaginary. The absolute perfection. Some even call it the most beautiful. Some others do not know what to call it, or what to think of it. A remnant of the sky? A piece of earth mimicking paradise? That is a place for reconciliation. Of nature with nature. Of people with life. Inexplicable.

Lagoa do Fogo - The triumph of water over fire. And the silence.

Lagoa do Fogo - the quintessential total serenity amidst a wild and fascinating frame

THERE IS MORE WATER IN THE LANDSCAPE

Water! No painter is ever indifferent to it. The water is the beginning and the end of any landscape. It recreates colours and forms around itself. It is like a poppy in a wheat field: whenever present it is always the centrefold. Be it in the forest with a rivulet or when a flower with a drop of water becomes a droplet in a flower.

Water is a constant presence all over S. Miguel. When it cannot be seen, then, its own child the green comes out. Jumping from a waterfall, hopping on the pebbles of a creek, restful on a lagoon, boiling inside the "cauldron" at Furnas or at Ribeira Grande. With all

those shapes and semblances in the seas that belong to any island the size of this. As island like this is no more than sea interruptus.

The traveller always keeps a lagoon well tucked inside his affection box, so well kept by Mother Nature that very few can visit it. In this case, it is the Congro Lagoon, "halfway on the way to Vila", going from Achada das Furnas to the road to Vila Franca. Its name originates on its owner, a man so wealthy that they called him Congro (conger eel), because it was considered the biggest fish in the seas, so said Frutuoso. It is located at the bottom of a crater that seems to have been drawn with compasses. Its scarped banks are covered by thick forest, so thick that no bird nest could be safer. One of nature's exquisite daintiness, right in the middle of the island's most active geological fault. Its name derives from this lagoon and from Fogo's. It was close to the latter

Here, quite often the water is coloured. Blue as the skies, green as the scenery or pink as the iron.

that they built a geothermal power plant, which supplies forty percent of all energy needs of the island. Next to it, what remains of a small-eutrophicated lagoon, an aquatic water-lily garden, which at his most splendorous moments was an impressionist vision of pink, yellow and white.

For those who enjoy the simple things in life, there is yet another lagoon not to be missed, as advised by the traveller. It is the St Brás Lagoon, accessible by a nice road, starting almost opposite the famous Gorreana Tea Factory. The words are worn, said again and again, but with a proven usage since they are truthful, and the traveller cannot find an advantageous replacement for it: bucolic. We mean the landscape. Trees on one side and pastures on the other. The sound of water caresses the grasslike rush and birds sing to life.

The contrast between **Salto do Cabrito** (Kids Goat Jump) and the bucolic serenity of **São Brás Lake**.

VILA FRANCA DO CAMPO
IT ALL BEGUN HERE

There are things and animals that occupy the landscape as if they belonged to it from the beginning of time. Or, as if they were remnants of the original paradise on earth: trees on single file on the horizon over the summit line, as children's drawings. Frightened rabbits crossing the road in search of their evening meal. Unhurried blackbirds returning home at twilight. Small cluster of old houses in the background.

That is how the traveller always envisioned one of these places suddenly revealed after a bend of the road. It is a small place called Praia (Beach), at the Parish of Água de Alto. No more than twenty houses or even less nestled between two ravines flanking the creek that drains out the surplus water from the Fogo Lagoon. One could not find a better postcard when walking in from the west into the Vila Franca do Campo County.

Vila Franca was the maiden municipality of the island. The south coast had the first settlement, the first town and the first city. Curiously, the first settlement was not the first town and the first town was not the first city. The primacy of Vila Franca do Campo would be lost on the ruins that almost wiped it out, by the time of the big landslide caused by the earthquake of October 22, 1522. When this happened, the town was already almost half a century old and it was the administrative head of the entire island of S. Miguel.

After the tragedy, it had to start from scratch. Whenever he cans, the traveller walks into the beautiful Mother Church, a symbol of that new beginning, that fierce will to remain where the heart is. It is a symbol since it was rebuilt as a replica of the temple buried under the mud. It expresses the belief that men did not feel alone amidst the desolation of such valley of tears. The tower and façade remind us of the old and ascetic roman architecture with gothic

Lugar da Praia, Água de Alto - Time has stopped in this idyllic recess, as if in a protest against the excesses of civilisation.

The **Cathedral of São Miguel** (St Michael) is a magnificent example of art and faith.

incrustations adorning the door. Inside, various altars and decorative motifs may look redundant or delirious. Indeed, they are an extraordinary aesthetical and mystical show. Around it grew a graceful and airy town, with a touch of Renaissance in its proportions and in the street design. Not much was left after the terrible earthquake, today known as subversion of Vila Franca. In the parish of S. Pedro (St Peter's) immediately afterwards, they built a small chapel

dedicated to Our Lady of the Rosary. Perhaps the current lent pilgrimage originated in the prayers then said at that chapel.

Vila Franca inherited from centuries past a religious architecture that, as usual here or anywhere else in Europe, is always the best. In those ancient times, humankind had not yet replaced God for lesser gods. Just opposite the Mother Church of S. Miguel Arcanjo (St Michael, the Archangel) the Hospital of

One of the many faces of Vila Franca do Campo, one of the most beautiful Azorean towns with its **islet** standing as a sentry.

Misericórdia (Mercy Hospital) and its annex church of Espírito Santo (the Holy Spirit), bear witness to Christian charity. They venerate the image of Senhor Bom Jesus da Pedra (Our Lord Jesus of the Rock). In its homage, they celebrate one of the biggest religious feasts of the island during the last weekend of August. What remains - the locutory and the church - from the Santo André (St Andrew's) Convent are some woods smelling of four centuries of history. Another pilgrimage place is the Little Chapel of Nossa Senhora da Paz (Our Lady of Peace) for believers or mere lovers of great landscapes. It must be noted that a tree may also be a monument. In the Antero do Quental Garden by the Mother Church, Misericórdia and the Town Hall, a tree is also a monument. A dragon tree was planted there the day HRH King Luis married on October 6, 1862.

Ponta Garça, the most populous parish on the district is famously known throughout the island for its length. It is more than a league long from one side to the other. Each year, the procession in honour of its

Vila Franca's Islet is a masterpiece of volcanic geometry.

patron, Nossa Senhora da Piedade (Our Lady of Piety), has to interchange its route, one year it goes westwards, the other year eastwards. This county has a continuous succession of houses, row after row. From Ponta Garça one moves onto Ribeira das Tainhas, and from here to Ribeira Seca, then to Vila and from Vila to Água de Alto.

All these places deserve a lengthy glimpse. Nearby, there are beaches with huge affluence of people such as Água de Alto and Vinha da Areia. Or, that natural prodigious event, the natural swimming-pool at the islet of Vila Franca do Campo. It is what remains from a crater of an extinct volcano, a mere kilometre from the shore with 150 metres in diameter. It is part, together with its maritime surroundings, of a Natural Reserve Park.

Right in the heart of Vila Franca. The **Church of Misericórdia** (Mercy Church)

A centuries- old garden with a Dragon tree planted on the day HRH King Dom Luís wed.

The **Little Chapel of Nossa Senhora da Paz** (Our Lady of Peace) is halfway between earth and sky.

The joy of the **Marches of São João** (St John parades)

Town Hall and a statue honouring **Gonçalo Vaz Botelho**, the town founder

Pottery is a tradition very much linked to the clay from Santa Maria Island, imported through Vila Franca.

The **Congro Lake** was thus named in honour of its former owner during the times of the first colonisation. Maybe it remains almost immaculate and virginal due to its difficult access.

The **South Coast** is fairly rich in fish and its seas are calmer. Beaches are more frequent and normally sheltered.

LAGOA

A traveller is led to believe that were Lagoa a kingdom, then Caloura would be the jewel in the crown. A jewel in a county that seemed destined to be of minor relevance. Lagoa is practically at the doorsteps of Ponta Delgada. In an island of this size, Ponta Delgada is capable of transforming the neighbouring towns in its satellites. This one, however, did not let itself be drained by the gravitational attraction of its neighbour, the biggest city of the archipelago. It has created its own life. Its industry was always innovative and active. Even when it pretended to be no more than utilitarian, with its earthenware or its recycled paper factory.

A traveller is happy to walk and stay over in this town. Free of the asphyxiating stress of great hurries. Free to contemplate the contour of the coastal line, or the design of its streets and the clearness of its urbanism. The traveller was being compelled to mention that the county of Lagoa is unique in the Azores, having two towns. Fortunately, he remembered that at Calheta, São Jorge Island, there are also two, Calheta and Topo. Walking eastwards you will find the other town, Água de Pau. Although both are ancient, the latter is even older than the head of the administrative division. After a period of huge economic development, Água de Pau baulked at the lack of natural resources and its municipality was extinguished. It has, nevertheless, kept and even reacquired the dignity of its noble origins. As well as a noble character. In case you did not know that, a village can also have character. It reflects the ways of being of its people. Here, one also has niches and recesses to

Old village, head of an administrative district until the 19th century

explore slowly. It is a pleasure to wander by.
The jewel on the crown belongs to Água de Pau. Caloura. The landscape suddenly changes as if not a part of the same island.
The traveller dreams of writing in a manner that the words would go unnoticed. As music from a violin without the sound, neither of the arch nor of the fingers jumping on the strings. As a pure white linen cloth table, free of renderings or embroideries. A plain tablecloth just sitting on top of the table so that everyone will notice the cutlery. The traveller is mostly fascinated by the harbour, filled with overwhelming memories of the lava, which created such a space. On its side, the first female convent of the Azores. There, it landed the effigy of Senhor Santo Cristo dos Milagres (Saint Christ of Miracles). God only knows how or where it came from, as a shipwreck or according to the legend coming from the seas. According to the history and not as legendary as the legend itself, it was proffered by Pope Paul III to a couple of young novices who went to Rome asking permission to create the monastery. Not afar from it,

Pottery is the most famous arts and crafts in Lagoa, reaching pure perfection. This sometimes buries excellent artists of aesthetic or other useful works. The **Presépio Museum** (Christmas Scenes Museum) keeps some of the most beautiful and popular works which came out of the able hands of its artisans.

only separated by walls, made up of stones, one on top of the other, there it is: the almost impossible Art Museum of the Caloura Cultural Centre.
The traveller spreads the plain tablecloth of the rustic linen of his words. The banquet is ready for your eyes. Once you walk into the Lagoa County and until the moment you depart at Ribeira Chã. Or, the other way round. A journey that one is led to embrace looking backwards to see the landscape grow and grow.

Caloura (its harbour and the Convent of Nossa Senhora da Conceição (Our Lady of the Conception) is one of the mythical places in São Miguel. Its good wine made it famous and the Cultural Centre (just behind the Convent) increased its prestige.

By Royal decision, **Carneiros Harbour**, in the quiet seas of Lagoa, was the one serving Ribeira Grande since there were no other sheltered ones nearby.

Gluttony kills more than the sword,
but many people depend on it to live

Ribeira Chã is a small hamlet worth visiting, not only because of its old harmony between landscape and population. Its Church is a magnificent example of modern art, and its Agricultural Museum draws our attention to old times and old survival techniques. *(Left, Top)*

Life goes on at the slow rhythm of a horse's walk *(Left, Center)*

PD615L
NOSSOGANHAPÃO

PONTA DELGADA

Ponta Delgada is an old and beautiful city. The traveller is led to believe it grew up, or tried to grow up, too quickly. It is a common problem faced by all cities, which are the most important regional centres. All innovations and anything new

had to happen there. Quite often wasting no time to make adjustments. Initially, Ponta Delgada tried to grow from the inside, an old and beautiful city that the 20th century did not respect.

The new went side by side with the old. Or even worse, the old came down to be replaced by the new. Merchants were very important in the old Ponta Delgada; they even got a very old street dedicated to them. The historical centre was the paradise where they could sell and trade. The essential life of the city moved to the outskirts, after the siege of big department stores and the turmoil created by living in half a dozen streets conceived for carriages and wagons. That type of Arab market of closed ceilings, gravitating close to the Mother Church moved away to the great fortresses of concrete and steel where there have shops for everything.

From ready to wear to ready to eat.
The traveller feels Ponta Delgada as a living being. The Immaculate Conception nights were a full splendour of light and creativity in dozens of shop windows daringly decorated to commemorate the day of urban commerce. Nowadays, bar a few exceptions, they are a sad chant incapable of disguising it. Its life went from inside to the outside. Now,

Town Hall Plaza with its imposing **statue of St Michael the Archangel** created by Numídico Bessone, the sculptor from Lagoa.

The Old **Misericórdia Hospital**, sits next to one of the biggest and most beautiful Azorean temples, the church of the old **Convent of São Francisco** (St Francis Convent)

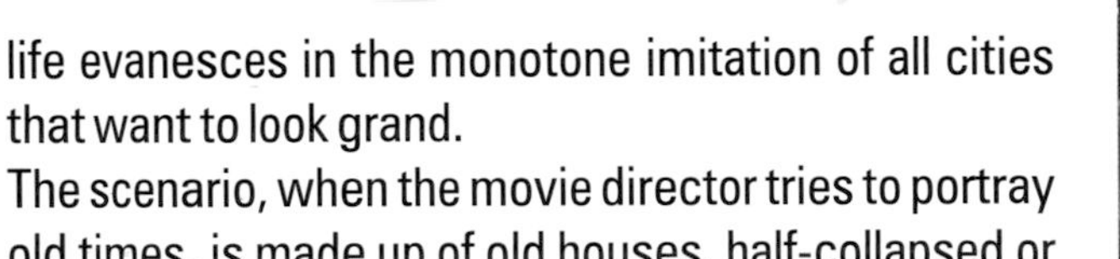

life evanesces in the monotone imitation of all cities that want to look grand.
The scenario, when the movie director tries to portray old times, is made up of old houses, half-collapsed or colour faded. However, in those old times, such houses would indeed be complete in every respect with shining and new colours. Ponta Delgada did not collapse nor faded its colours. It was forced to give up being what it was. Now, meaning the past decades, there is no make-up capable of returning the old dame to its ancestral good looks. The urge to enchase novelty was taken to the utmost of removing, stone by stone, the Little Chapel of Trindade (Trinity) to the entrance of the António Borges Garden. The old setting is now occupied by a petrol station.
However, there is still plenty to be seen in Ponta Delgada, plenty to love. The traveller, who could never draw, attended High School there proving that he knew the other subjects more or less well. There, h also tried to learn the difficult art of teaching. He tried to complete his studies with divine intervention, as so many who used to do, going to pray on their knees at the doorsteps of the Church of the Convent of

The **São Sebastião Mother Church** (St Sebastian) has amassed centuries and different architectonic styles.

Charabanc (carriage with wooden benches) was the means of transportation for wealthy families. Today is no more than a trip to the past.

The **Plaza of São Francisco** (St Francis) is as old as its first inhabitants.

Esperança (Hope). Many also left a message pencilled on the green panelled door so that the Lord did not forget their prayers. "Dear Senhor Santo Cristo dos Milagres (Christ of Miracles) help me with the French test." "Christ of Miracles help me on maths." And so many other requests. Others were of a more distressed kind, of life or death.

. There is an old devotion to this Christ of Miracles. Its beautiful icon came from the Convent of Caloura. Its feast is nowadays the biggest of these islands after an initial procession, back in 1698, visiting other Convents in Ponta Delgada. The church is equally beautiful. The church of S. José (Saint Joseph), on the western side of the Mall, used to be part of the Franciscan Convent. It is a monument of large proportions and magnificent altars.

Temples and old convents everywhere in these islands are always the most interesting places to visit. The Church of the Jesuits' College is now converted into a Museum of Sacred Art. Some of the

altars are missing, one of them was offered to the Santa Luzia Church at Feteiras do Sul, as a reward prize for some election that the Regeneration Party won there in the 1800's. Nevertheless, the carved work is fascinatingly exuberant. The College has been turned into a Public Library. On the eastern side of the mall there is another baroque monument, the Church of S. Pedro (St Peter), turned into Royal Chapel, while HRH Pedro IV was in the island. There is also the Convent of Santo André (St Andrew), made a general museum but with notable collections of paintings and natural history. The traveller feels fascinated by the High Choir of its church, daydrea-

The **Palace of the Baron of Fonte Bela** served as Ponta Delgada's first High School. Today it continues its function as a secondary school.

The **Conceição Palace** serves as host for various offices of the Regional Government of the Azores.

If all churches defer to the Mother Church,
the **Jesuit's College Church** transmuted in Sacred Art Museum
is one of the most extraordinary examples
of Portuguese Baroque Art.

The **Church of S. Pedro** (St Peter's) is another nice illustration of baroque, and it was once a Royal Chapel while HRH king Dom Pedro IV stayed in Ponta Delgada.

The **Mother Church** from another angle

The **Church of the Convent of Esperança** where the Senhor Santo Cristo dos Milagres (Saint Christ of Miracles) image is revered is a Diocesan Sanctuary.

The fascinating **image of Saint Christ** during the procession, one of the biggest shows of worship by the faithful in Portugal.

The **Hill of Mãe de Deus** (Mother of God) was not only a place of devotion to the Virgin Mary.
It was also used for the defence of Ponta Delgada.

Market abundance with fruits from soil.

Created by a lavic eccentricity, the **Carvão (Coal) Cave** goes for over a kilometre under Ponta Delgada subsoil.
(Left, Bottom)

ming of that space of gold and mystery.
When one travels in no hurries and without a map, one can still find some pleasant surprises. A very old lane which has remained impervious to the passage of time, a manor house from the wealthy times of orange exports, responsible for fortunes and barons, or a small niche belonging to a country village and sneaked into town, without losing the rustic appearance of its people or houses.
Southwards, Ponta Delgada has lost most of its character after 1940. The Estado Novo (Portuguese for "New State") wanted to show its influence and robbed the sea of enough space to create one more mall and a new avenue, where previously there was an embarking pier. Malls and Avenues were some of the trademarks of the regime's propaganda. Afterwards, they could not devise a retrocession for the metamorphosis. Or, at least, to stop it. They even land filled one of the most expressive memories of Ponta Delgada, the Calheta de Pêro de

The **Military Museum** keeps
memories of bravery and sufferance

Teive, a fishermen's place from immemorial times. The new avenue ended up accepting a bit of everything. Epoch styles and architectural styles. Each of them more interested in his scale models than looking around. When the night comes, the light show ends up giving a strange beauty to that place. As if rehabilitating it, or justifying it. From the S. Brás Fortress to the modern Cruise Pier at Portas do Mar (Sea Gates), where ships bring in people from all over the world. They can only depart with good mementos from this city. if only the soul could serve as a tour guide.

The **Theatre and the Coliseum Micaelense**
are nice and functional buildings
attesting to the cultural vitality of Ponta Delgada

The **António Borges Garden**
is one of many heritages from the 19th century.

The garden in front of the 16th century S. Brás Fortress
(Center)

The **marina** is a door ajar to sailors from all over the world

The **seaside avenue** (or Infante Dom Henrique Avenue) is the public promenade of all summer nights.

Portas do Mar (Sea Gateways) open the island to visitors arriving by sea

Portas da Cidade (Town Gates) are a monument meaning but a remembrance of the past. In order to give passage to the seaside avenue they were forced to be moved back a few yards.

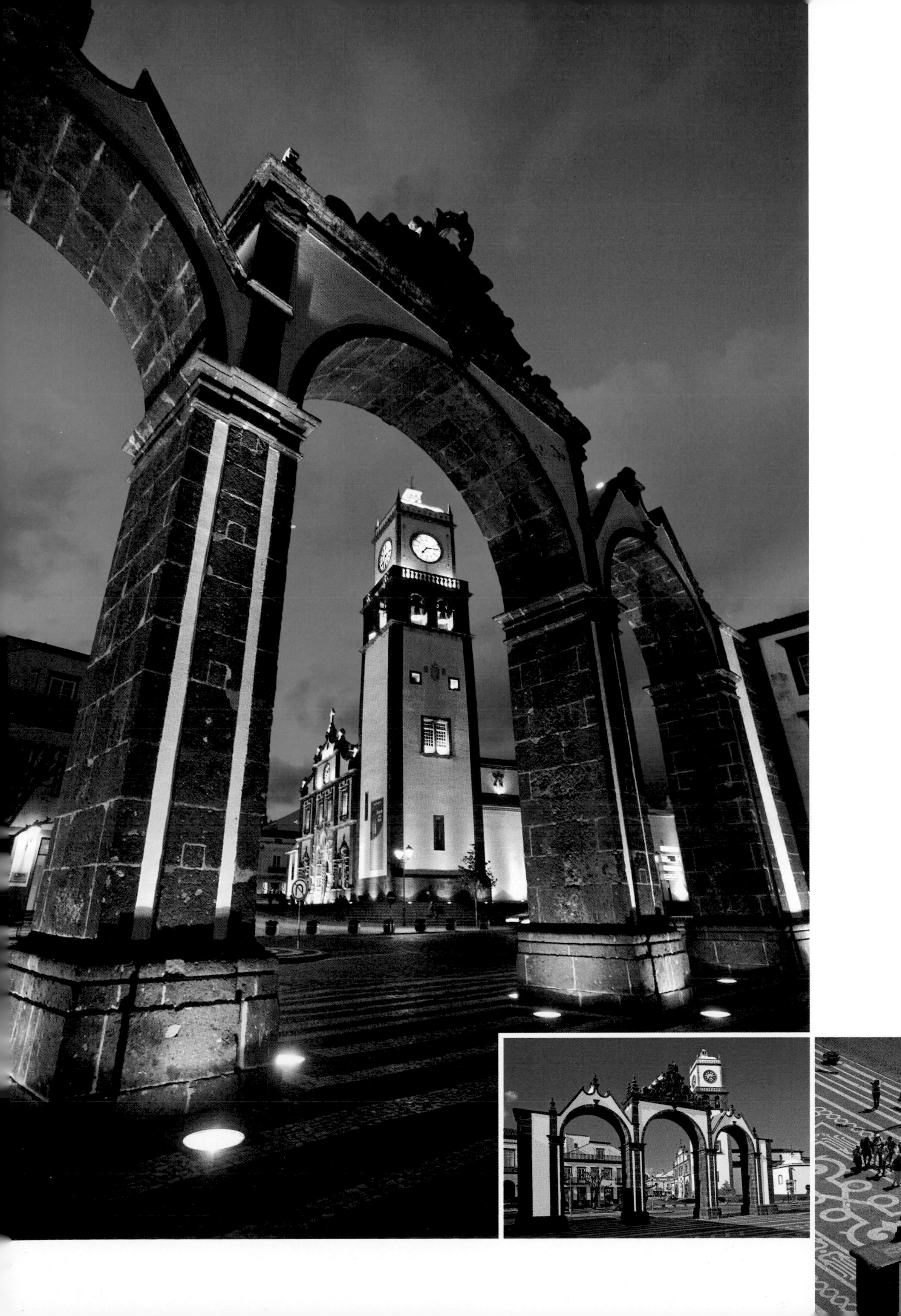

THE BIG COUNTY (PONTA DELGADA)

The traveller knows that smells supplement the landscape colours, as colours do complete the forms. The smell, of all those yesteryear smells long gone, the one he misses most is that from the wheat fields. A warm smell in anticipation of oven bread. A sensual smell on the waves of brunette ears of corn, splashed by incandescent poppies as signs of virginity. The perfect environment for forbidden loves or ashamed ones.

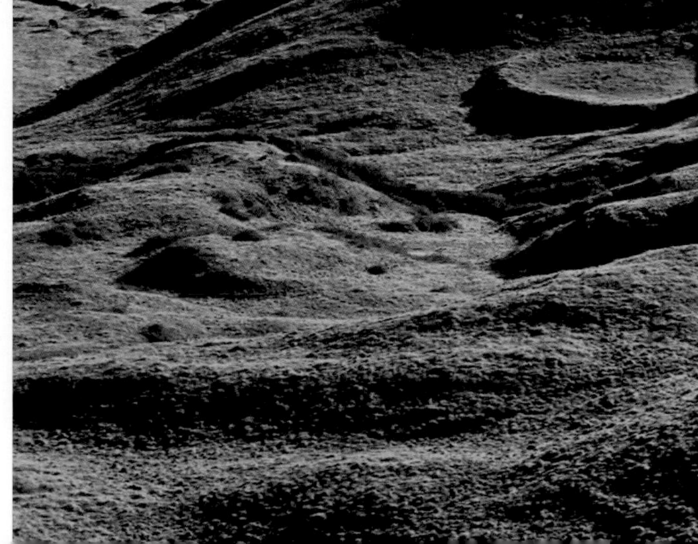

The traveller keeps these mementos from the largest county in the Azores, especially from around the Feteiras do Sul, where he keeps family and affection. Close by the church of Santa Luzia, the one whose altar and pulpit were brought from the Jesuit Church College.
Harvesting and husking were festivals of joy and fraternity. Ox-carts would come announced in the distance by their plaintive squeaky axles. Everything looked démodé but nothing was sad. Not even the following parish, Candelária, considered by its priest as the island's poorest at the turn of the 19th century. Perhaps it was. It might not have changed a lot for the best part of seven decades, but suddenly, from night to day, became filled up with new colours and cultural movements, starting to extract from its soil more than the wheat, long gone, or the excessive milk. Its name became a trademark of tastes treasured by the whole island.
After Candelária, comes Ginetes, which advances almost up to Ponta da

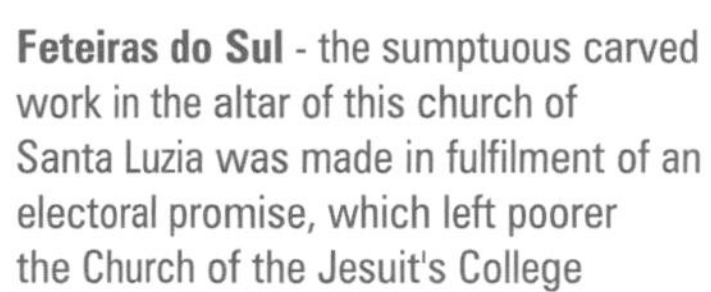

Feteiras do Sul - the sumptuous carved work in the altar of this church of Santa Luzia was made in fulfilment of an electoral promise, which left poorer the Church of the Jesuit's College

Candelária - during the first decades of the 20th century, Candelária was considered one of the most laid back parishes in São Miguel Island. These days it is one of the most progressive both in cultural and economic terms. here one can witness a procession honouring its patron Our Lady of Candelária (or Our Lady of Candles)

Feteiras do Sul - after the prayers in the temple, a ranch of pilgrims in front of the parish of Santa Luzia, protector of the vision.

Ferraria, where there is an almost natural museum of vulcanology. One gets to Várzea, always going around the massif of Sete Cidades (Seven Cities), before descending to the Mosteiros (Monasteries) in a fajã[3] of capricious indentation. It is surrounded by a sea which provided its share of fame due to octopus and barnacles (locally known as cracas).

After Mosteiros one is already on the North Coast. The landscape seems to reinvent itself after each bend of the road, remade on the relief and the look of the vegetation. Bretanha, Remédios, Santo António... Even the sounds, especially in Bretanha, resemble the sounds of France that legend has it as

Ponta da Ferraria - the unexpected show of a lighthouse amidst the pasturelands
(Top, Center)

Walking slowly, living in no hurries
(Top, Right)

Ponta da Ferraria - a natural geological atlas
(Center, Left)

This is the water they drink in Ponta Delgada
(Bottom, Right)

[3]flat lowland areas formed by lava flowing into the ocean and landslides and collapsing cliffs.

Capelas - they keep the noble air of its status as a village.
Its harbour is one of the most ravishing of this island

Mosteiros - these islets gave name to a beautiful village spreading through a volcanic fajã.

the origin of its first inhabitants. With royal blood, so they say.
At the village of Capelas one should not be distracted by the magnificent mess created by houses and woods. One cannot miss the trip to the Belvedere. Many a sperm whale was spotted from there when whale hunting was one of the island's riches. Its cliffs have an impressive and ravishing beauty. The county ends up at Fenais da Luz, although it continues inland with the most hinterland parish of the island at S. Vicente.
Almost nothing separates the suburbs from the city of Ponta Delgada. It spreads to Relva, where the airport is located; and to Arrifes and Covoada, one of the largest milk producing areas n the Azores; it spreads to Fajãs – Fajã de Cima and Fajã de Baixo. Then, eastwards there is S. Roque and Livramento, with their popular black sand beaches still protected by the ruins of antique fortresses that no one knew how to preserve. As so many others throughout the island.

You get in no hurry to leave and go, do you?

São Roque, a rock that becomes an islet during high tides. A church that is a lighthouse for the faithful and a reference for the men at sea.

A village right in the city?

Swordfish is not known for an easy surrender and in the Azorean seas some specimen can be caught after many hours of struggle

Batalha - It may not look like it, but the golf course at Batalha was crated in one of the most arid corners of the island

There is always he sea where dolphins and people play

Lagoa de São Tiago - Gaspar Frutuoso said that in this lake a certain type of fish was found almost like a prawn. Who knows if the Louisiana crayfish (Procambarus clarkii) just recently discovered wasn't already here?

Sete Cidades - Sete Cidades (Seven Cities) - one can never escape the fascination of these Siamese lakes. Each recess is a moment of perfect tranquillity and beauty. Even the causeway, separating the green from the blue lakes, is as naturally there as the common alder and the maple ash

RIBEIRA GRANDE

Ribeira Grande (Great Creek). The traveller has spent there quite some time. Every single day of the week but Sundays. It was there that he attended the External Day-School to learn some Letters and a few other Sciences. Lunch was always taken in the lane where Gaspar Frutuoso might have walked a million times, on his way to the Mother Church of Nossa Senhora da Estrela (Our Lady of the Stars) where he was vicar. A sage man, a doctorate in Theology by the University of Salamanca he

has left us the biggest and almost unique pages of History known about the first years of settlement of these islands. At the majestic Town Hall Chambers, a wall mural dedicated to him has always intrigued the traveller. The priest is seen on the tiles preaching from the pulpit of his Church. Also present in that panel some agricultural implements and symbols of the art of writing with these words as motto: "If I knew, I would not have known". Easy to interpret... Had Frutuoso learned the

The town of Ribeira Grande and neighbouring parishes lie on a very fertile and extremely beautiful vast open plain

These colourful houses at the mouth of Ribeira Grande are reminiscent of a Maluda painting

arts and skills of caring for the land and he would not have known the other art of writing. May be not, who is there to know? What if that was a confession? That if he knew what constitutes noesis he would have preferred not knowing? That cognition that makes us more conscious of our own ignorance. More insatiable. That knowledge which makes us doubt more than believing in what we learn.

The traveller is often tempted by it. As a regret for having learned more than all the other kids from his homeland who have gone to the baptismal font the same year he did. Thank God, that Gaspar Frutuoso had learned other wisdoms, instead of learning of plough and weeding hoes. Because he was the only one to tell us things that, if it were not for him, no one would know about. The traveller, however, has never learned more that already known wisdoms. His words are not even crucial for a visit. To fill one's eyes with the surrounding world. To this traveller or to any other traveller it is enough to go up there and watch. The dance of the seagulls in the indescribable Fogo Lagoon. On its way up, the cascade of hot waters at Caldeira Velha (Old Cauldron). The other

The much degraded space of old Cova do Milho (Corn Cove), currently the **Jardim do Paraíso** (Paradise Garden) became one of the nicest spots in Ribeira Grande

The **Town Hall**, this building, started in the 17th century was concluded in the 18th century

The **Mother Church Nossa Senhora da Estrela** (Our Lady of the Stars) is one of the most beautiful and widest Azorean temples *(Bottom, Left)*

The exuberant baroque style of the **old Church of Misericórdia** (Mercy) *(Bottom, Center)*

In the **Waterfall Plaza**, an aesthetic dialogue takes place between basalt and limestone *(Bottom, Right)*

One feels blessed by the overpowering scenery
and the gift of eyesight when admiring **Lagoa do Fogo** (Lagoon of Fire or Fire Lake)

The landscape is dazzling on the way to the Lagoa do Fogo (Lagoon of Fire or Fire Lake) with astonishing details such as the **Caldeira Velha** (Old Springs) and its surrounding foliage

The **Ribeiragrandense Theatre** is a marvellous cultural space where anything can happen, from musical concerts to conferences and film screenings

Santa Barbara sand beach and the **Poças da Ribeira Grande** (pools) are a couple of places where people again meet the sea

fumaroles so called Caldeiras da Ribeira Grande (Ribeira Grande Cauldrons). The baroque boulders at Lombadas, with its magnificent spring of mineral water. The astonishment of Monte Escuro (Dark Mount). There, where the land has not had the time to disguise the hands of fire from its volcanoes. The silence almost muffles one's mouth although there is so much to glimpse from up there. Speaking becomes forbidden. There is a certain place where one can clearly see a barely heard waterfall. If one lowers the eyes behind some queirós (Calluna vulgaris, heather), rachitic at that altitude, nothing can be heard. Further ahead, there are sensations apiece. The Ponta do Cintrão (Cintrão Point) is a daring miniaturesque Cape; Santa Iria Belvedere where one suddenly discovers as the island keeps unfolding, small fingers of land getting into the sea, or those dalliances of the sea in the coves. That is the place where the traveller always makes a gazebo for History. In its surroundings hills took place the largest and last engagement between the Absolutist troops and the liberals who had earlier disembarked at Achadinha in early 19th century. Porto Formoso (Handsome Harbour) is just in front with its beach, considered the best

anchoring harbour of the northern coast. Then, the rutilant São Brás; and Maia, in a volcanic "fajã" where the sun is least absent and the weather is more temperate than any of its surroundings. Afterwards comes Lomba da Maia and Fenais da Ajuda, whose elegant Point announces the end of the county, further up at Lomba de São Pedro.

The traveller has also walked into, and stayed numerous times, the Church of Nossa Senhora da Estrela (Our Lady of the Stars) at Ribeira Grande. Even to this day, when returning there, he feels a sense of respectful fright. It is one of the biggest temples in the Azores. It is said that

This **fountain at Ribeira Seca** was buried by the volcanic eruption of 1563

Ponta do Cintrão or Cape Cintrão is just one of many headlands that can be observed from the **Santa Iria Belvedere** where the horizon is almost endless

Rabo de Peixe (literally Fish Tails) is renowned by its famous fishermen as dedicated sea wolves

Maia is a volcanic fajã dating back ten thousand years and for the past half millennium one of the most remarkable villages in the county and the island

similar ones are only the Angra Cathedral and the São José Church (St Joseph's) at Ponta Delgada. The Christian devotion in past times is well represented in the cornucopia of its altars. Its art is also obvious in abundant ornamentation. There is kept the Arcano Místico (Mystical Arcane), a work by Mother Margarida do Apocalipse (Margaret of the Apocalypse). The traveller is now told that one of these days it will be transferred to the house where she lived, since the Liberals then closed the doors of the Convent where she and others lived.

It was in that side of the creek that Ribeira Grande started growing during the 14th century. When HRH King Manuel I promoted it to a town on August 4, 1507, he defined its borders as being within a league from the pillory. In the 19th century, the county attained its current dimension.

Until it was elevated to City in 1981, Ribeira Grande had only two parishes, Matriz (Cathedral) and Conceição. At that historic moment, it gained the parishes of Ribeira Seca (Dry Creek) and Ribeirinha (Little Creek), and, later on, Santa Bárbara.

A further league to its western side, there is Rabo de Peixe (Fish Tails), a parish promoted to town on April 25, 2004. It is the most populous and contrary to its opposite fame, is also one of the richest. Its fishing harbour is one of the most important in the Azores. It also has superior quality fruits and horticultural products. The old airport was located in this parish, a mere pasture where cows fed when the planes were not around. Further ahead, there is Calhetas, and further away, only half a dozen kilometres from Ponta Delgada, you have Pico da Pedra (Stone Peak). Its landscape is one of the most recent in geological terms. If everything were as it was, 50,000 years, a mere split second in Earth's Evolution, one would have no soil where to put his feet. In those days, there was only sea between the Sete Cidades massif and the Água de Pau Mountain.

The **Cavalhadas at Ribeira Seca** (horse tournaments evoking the battles between Christian and Moors) are horse parades in honour of the saint patron, St Peter. They revere the first agricultural production and possibly worship God for having spared from certain death the inhabitants of the island during the terrible volcanic crisis of 1563

During the celebration of the **Holy Ghost Festival at Maia**, patron of the local parish, more than three thousand people sit at the fraternity table

Lomba da Maia did belong to Maia until the first half of the 20th century. It is one of the biggest milk producing parishes in the island

Tea is the most universal drink and is blessed by its antioxidant characteristics protecting the heart and fighting cancer. The **Gorreana Tea Factory** is the only one still in production from its inception in 1883 till today

Somewhat lacking historical validity,
these are remarkable manifestations
of popular customs at the intoxicating landscape
where the **Tea Factory of Porto Formoso** is located

The **Church of the Saint Magi of Fenais da Ajuda**,
a place inhabited and first populated
at the same time as Porto Formoso and Maia

Porto Formoso has been a parish of
Nossa Senhora da Graça (Our Lady of Grace)
since the turnaround of the 15th century.
Its natural harbour made this a unique place and the
only one in the northern coast of São Miguel Island
to be mapped five hundred years ago

"THE ARCHAEOLOGY OF THE SILENCE"

(TITLE OF AN EDITORIAL BY JOSÉ RICARDO COSTA, IN **JORNAL TORREJANO**)

The traveller sums up the balance of its journey. The best are the travels that do not end when one reaches the final destination. They force us to return to the trails of their memory. Yet again past and present are intertwined. Are they worthy of their time or by themselves? Could today's poetic sounds be the rattle of a motor engine as half a century ago it was the creaking wheels of an ox-cart? Could the beauty of concrete architecture have the same sentimental value of a stone house with a door and two small windows? Could a painter have the same feelings towards a green prairie and a poppy field? Do they still have the same flavour, the bread, the Portuguese sweet bread known as massa sovada, malassadas[4], goat cheese, blackberry jam, sweet potatoes or oven-roasted pumpkin? And does the forage change the taste of eggs or the pork in torresmos de vinha de alhos[5], the chorizo sausage and morcelas[6]?

The traveller does not sum up the balance of this journey. The traveller cogitates. He is standing up at Santa Iria Belvedere. He read about someone who spoke on the archaeology of silence. That impossible attempt to extract from the past sounds that only last a few seconds

What astounding sounds could then be heard around those hills! What blasts and cries from a battle without a general rehearsal? A battle where you kill and get killed as it happened when the liberals and absolutists got together there[7].

Throughout that coast it seems that the island feels sorry for becoming this end of the land elongated in successive capes ahead. At that distance, the Tronqueira Mountain looses its wild albeit indomitable aspect. The traveller never looks at Vara Peak, even from this distance afar, never forgetting Ginette Neveu and the silence created for her Stradivarius violin. Or Edith Piaf's heart dilacerated by the shattered body of Marcel Cerdan.

The mountains have always charged their toll for their

[4]fried kneaded dough

rights of passage. These have been no more rapacious than many others. People lost on them. Travellers on foot or air travellers like those from Air France, close by Algarvia, as young Marc Philip, who just missed by a dozen metres the flight over Barrosa Peak. But these mountains are always the most beautiful landmarks of the landscape. Even if they are hurt by the geothermal towers that create more than 40% of all energy consumed by the island.

Can one only imagine the island six centuries ago when seen by the first immigrants? We should leave that revelation lost in the eternal silence of a supposed Diogo, or Diego, and those sailors they commanded.

The traveller suspends its balance of the journey to

[5] spareribs in a garlic wine and pepper sauce

[6] blood sausages

ponder about those old times. It must have been the starting point of the island for European eyes. Some others even accept the theory of the Phoenicians having been here before Christ birth but Phoenicians were no more than seafaring sailors, and in those days it would be unconceivable to risk a voyage to the unknown and immense sea. People even believe they have charted all of Africa but they should have sailed close by the coast and if the Normans have reached the Americas at the turn of the 10th century, landing first at Greenland it was only a small trip when compared to a trip from Lisbon or Lagos till the Azores. The Normans had already scaled the Faroe Islands and Iceland who had been inhabited by centuries in those days. From Iceland to Greenland the distance is only 300 km, or twice the distance between São Miguel and Terceira. With good visibility they might not even have lost sight of land. Halfway through them should have watched Iceland and even further, the Greenland.

What has supposedly seen Diogo, said of Silves but most surely not, and his sailors, was an island filled up with so thick vegetation that it was hard to go inland. Some of these species have already vanquished in Europe and yet here they are the mainstay of laurisilva forest with plenty of laurel (laurel nobilis). Some of its remnants can be found in the most inaccessible places, because the remainder has been slowly occupied by local agriculture. Firstly, dedicated to satiate hunger and to produce wheat to feed the soldiers of the North African fortresses and barley for horses. It also produced plenty of pastel with that sparkling blue so often painted by the Flemish artists.

The orange cycle came afterwards from the end of the 17th century until well after the first half of the 18th century. It was a time to create manor houses and barons. But it also created lots of poor people and immigrants in their own islands looking for farms where they could find work. The traveller guesses that perhaps a third of all arable soil was filled up with orange groves. That was the land that the poor people needed to grow what to eat. The legend has it that Marie Antoinette stated that if people had no bread let them eat cake, but in this island the abundance of oranges was such that children acquired a yellowish pallor due to the excess of citreous acid. Exports reached more than 150 million oranges in the last years of its abundance. That is when the Micaelense Society for Promotion of Agriculture was created. No other political or civic movement in the Azores was ever more important than this one. It was determinant

[7] Translator's Note: From 1826 to 1834 the Portuguese fought a civil war, known as the Liberal Wars or the Portuguese Civil War, the War of the Two Brothers, or Miguelite War) (Livermore, 1966; Vieira, 2004). Fought between the Liberals, under Pedro IV, at time King of Portugal and Emperor of the Brazil, and the Absolutists or Miguelistas after their leader Dom Miguel (Pedro's brother). The Liberals supported a Constitutional Monarchy, and their leader wanted to secure the Portuguese throne for his daughter Dona Maria II. The Absolutists, in contrast, believed in Miguel's divine right to rule

The **Navy school training ship Sagres**, a symbol of seafaring that revealed to the world this speck of land, an oasis in the middle of the Atlantic Ocean *(Top, Left)*

Santa Iria Belvedere - earth, ocean and skies *(Top, Center)*

Sete Cidades (Seven Cities) - A boulevard to meet God at His **Church of São Nicolau** (Saint Nicholas)

Ribeira Seca - **Mafoma Manor House** where the knights of Cavalhadas meet in honour of St Peter

Povoação - the old church dedicated to **Nossa Senhora dos Anjos** (Our Lady of the Angels)

Maia - a stretch of land between the ocean and the mounts

for the future of the islands with consequences that are still felt to this day. Men that were able to understand that the orange trade would not last forever. New means of transportation – steam boats and trains – would allow consumers in Northern Europe an easy access to oranges originating in Sicily or Valencia. Furthermore a deadly disease was already insinuating the destruction of the orange orchards. About three decades before such a wealth was destroyed the Society started thinking about possible solutions to that problem. Slowly, bit by bit, new experimental cultures were introduced. Pineapple, tea, tobacco, chicory and beetroot became the new democratic

wealth since everyone could benefit from their work even the poorest members of the society. It was also the time to start the reforestation of the island. Millions of boxes made up to carry between 800 and 1,000 oranges had almost depleted the island of worthy wood totally destroying the bushes of the Furnas valley. That explains how Cryptomeria japonica became so ambivalent in the island.

That group of benefactors was also responsible for the education of an almost medieval popular mentality when they founded the newspaper O Agricultor Micaelense, promoting the teaching of a mostly illiterate population.

São Miguel became a top destination in the Azores. Simultaneously, tourism started developing and that explains why today this island gets the highest number of tourists. It is (however) a false notion that São Miguel can be confused with the whole archipelago São Miguel does not comprise or sum up all the other islands. Each island has its very unique landscape and social characteristics which make them irrevocable. One has to assume the political definition of the archipelago as an autonomous region with a collective identification element. One has to benefit from the Micaelense dynamism, to develop the whole archipelago. Being here one is also close to Santa Maria, to Terceira, or even Flores and Corvo. Each island is a melting pot of emotional alchemies that are bound to awe anyone facing them.

Pico da Vara Peak - walking to the top where the island ends at a height of more than 1100 meters

Tea, **pineapple** and **hydrangeas** were all introduced in São Miguel island during the 19th century as a response to the crisis in the orange trade and a notable advancement of agriculture. A lesson well learned for nowadays

DANIEL DE SÁ

Daniel Augusto Raposo de Sá, was born in Maia, S. Miguel (Azores) on March 2, 1944. He completed his studies as a Primary School Teacher at the Higher School for Education (Escola do Magistério Primário) at Ponta Delgada, 1960-1062. Previously, attended the External School (Externato) at Santa Maria up to Year 4 and Year 5 of his High School Certificate at Ribeira Grande (Externato Ribeiragrandense). He graduated in Philosophy at the Faculty of Combonian Missionaries, Moncada, Valencia (Spain), having completed the first year of Theology at the Diocesan Seminary of Valencia (Spain) and attended year 2 at the Faculty of Theology in Granada (Spain).

His only professional occupation was Primary School Teacher. Daniel however had many political appointments: Regional Secretary (equivalent to Regional Director) of Social Communication and Sports of the Azores Regional Junta, being an elected member of Parliament in the first two legislative sessions of the Azores Autonomous Regional Assembly (local parliament), being an alderman at the Ribeira Grande Municipal Council, and also a member of the Ribeira Grande Municipal Assembly.

DEDICATED

To Calie
To the newborn baby Isabel, Marta and Tiago, so that one day they may know better the land where mother Carolina, mother Sara, uncle Rodrigo and Grandma Alice were born.

With this book, **Ver Açor** continues to unveil the vast Azorean heritage, namely in terms of culture, religion, architecture and landscape. To all those who have helped us achieve our goal goes our deepest gratitude.